Harmony Rude

Steven Mooney

ISBN: 978-1-7345356-2-4

Cover Image: Three Figures, Robert Broderson
with permission of the artist's estate

Oval Books, Chapel Hill

First Draft2Digital Edition

This book is for Dina Sumaylo Mooney and for good poet and good friend, Scott Lowery

Contents

doing Time

Time moves ever silent in its cadence
Offering no sense of peace or of patience
When the love of your life just disappears
Ghosted as unanswered prayers in arrears

Suffering with and without support's grace
Soothes only so much, the rest you just face
Alone in the night bereft of when, it seems
Your loved one's caress, you trace in dreams

And that is all you have. Evermore!
No body to intern
No husk to burn

There is only Love that Loves to the Core

{after the missing Malaysian Airlines fight}

Cantilevered Cant

Jack be nimble
    Jack be quick Jack
burned his ass as did Nick
    unguent ointment aloes
    did the trick

Lunchcounter orders where
   was at place?
   Oh yeah, King's Sandwich Shop
catty-corner old Bulls ballpark.
Order at the window
   what's her name in there
whispered the line "ass on fire,"
was it footloose or footlong
    Hold the relish!

    Listening on the bus
I caught I thought
    the black pepper pipeline and that
   coughed up the old Mission Rock Resort
standing at the bar how many
   listening the radio announcer
call the Giants game at just over there
   Hunter's Point at Windlestick
as Willie McCovey steps to the plate

2

in all ignorance of lovely
　　　derelict piers, rusted bollards, and a lost
directionless kid amid ghosted
steam freighters & trawler hawsers
　　roped up love Oh all so gone to
swirling fuzzy desolation

2025 Congressional Bile Pile Report

There's nothing too heinous
We will ever let stain us
    for he's our Boy!
We tow the line of science as sham
That climate change is a Chinese scam
    for he's our Boy!
And paying off that porno star muff
In our opinion didn't go far enough
    for he's our Boy!
Mass murder of the machinegun sort
Underlies the girder of our support
        for he's our Boy!
We all voted to overthrow an election
Faithful to our leader's dereliction
    for he's our Boy!
National security, well, we don't care that
He got some documents, hey, let's all share
    for he's our Boy!
We'll Maga-correct this country's flaws
By canceling rights and suborning laws
    for he's our Boy!

No boast is too vain, no act too vile, you

See, leadership isn't substance, it is style

      for he's our Boy!

The Constitution is just ancient screed (breath) a

Parchment foolscap we no longer need

      for he's our Boy!

Now that he's a convicted felon

We say that Law is the real villain

      for he's our Boy!

We'll just keep on playing dumb, when

Anyone talks about him we stay mum

As with the January Sixth violence, you

Won't goad we toadies from our silence

      for he's our Joy

Daniel Ellsberg

My 1960s wasn't all folk music and blues,
Nope, got caught up in slaughter reviews. I
Marched in protests to help us lose Vietnam!

My service to Peace was given in Tear Gas that
Occluded clear views of who or what but our
Clarity of gain was wholeheartedly undenied;

Today, one true hero of that time has died.

Moratoriums we marched were solemn parades, no
Brass band Oompah Sousa, silence was the rule to
Honor American voices lost in that holocaust.

Marches restored in us the essence of Thomas Paine,
And as avowed pacificists we received insults in train
Opposed to its war and to erase the national stain, for
By then hundreds of thousands of civilians had died!

       We are all guilty that
Johnson, McNamara, and tricky Dick Nixon had lied!

Today, one true hero of that time has passed,

Daniel Ellsberg, Rest in Peace, my brother

Dissolute Urbane

When Claude said, I'm soaking my feet again,

Belle halved an eggplant and then again before an

Otherwise ordinary erstwhile suburban ignore.

Dollar Bill

Look at the father of our country
first General on the roster,
first to stand up in a boat,
winter river crossing,
must have been an imposter

He couldn't be painted sitting
(just another rank-and-file Minute)
his tricorner knocking others
Excuse me, Excuse Me
echoes amid the floes
Shut yer yap, a sergeant blisters!
as the Boat Master whispers
    If only he'd stand up

Musket stocks in the armpits
muzzles amid the thwarts
beneath the greatcoat hid
crutches cross the Delaware
No mention made in Trenton

Duke & Edna's Sparkling Lug-tread Whitewalls
Kudos to Thomas McGuane's, Bushwacked Piano

Tire additives are killing fish. So what

Do we do? Drive to church to make a wish,

Gun in the holster another between the seats

As we gun the engine to blast the streets, then

Go about our busily nascent oft quaffed

Way of life.

But this

Trajectory of fish and reported climate spoil

Is a dish of someone else's burning salmon oil!

See here, the American Can-do attitude ain't

No platitude when we kick the can

Down the road, pop some caps in it

And then reload

    with Slogans!

Flintlock Membrane: An Immodest Proposal

Let's restrict civilian & non-hunting permit gun owners to

    The weapons used in the period in which the 2nd

Amendment to the United States Constitution was written
and so satisfy

    Why we are so smitten and vexed, if not (Yell this:

Hexed from taking a sentence out of its context!

    I'd go for it. You?

That amendment is itself out of step

    With the times,

Yet its context we hold to be true

    For *ALL TIME*. Thus, let us restrict

One flintlock musket per family member,

    Ditto one flintlock pistol,
  and for each a

Single sack of powder and a sack of Sack too!

    The framers could not have imagined

Gatling Guns of a century hence, much less today's

    Hand-held household garden-variety automatic

      Butchery tools turned loose daily on ourselves in

Places of worship and commerce, and in our schools!

Our forefathers knew nothing of machine guns.

What they meant by "arms" was the assault Weapon of
Concord and Lexington, of

Fort Ticonderoga and Breeds Hill; and later still of
Latter day Minutemen betrayed and made-poor farmer

Hellion in Daniel Shays Rebellion.

The "shot heard 'round the world'" was

One Shot!

(Not that staccato rip

from a banana clip)

Let us examine how the flintlock rifle is prepped for

the next Single Shot:

` Use a clean cloth to wipe the lock
` Check the flint for it must be sharp, if needed

knap a new edge (but don't try it in the dark)
` Use the vent prick to clear the touch hole
` Swab the barrel but don't use your shirt, use a

clean patch that's free of dirt
` Pull the lock to half cock
` Pinch a cartridge from the cartouche, bring it to your mouth after

oxygen debouche
` Tear the cartridge with your teeth (denture bearers

(may need relief)
` Pour priming powder to fill half the flash pan, away

from the touch hole (too much powder at the touch-
hole position may act like a fuse and slow ignition)

` Close the pan
` Stand the rifle on its stock with muzzle facing the sky
    (Don't look into the bore and don't ask why)
` Pour the charge down the barrel (powder measure)
` Start the ball down the muzzle over a lubricated patch
` Use the short starter first, long starter second, and the
    Ramrod to seat the ball firmly against the charge
` Set the hammer to full cock and take aim
` Squeeze the trigger and hold aim until the BLAST!

By such process, muskets will not muzzle
    Mass killings, but they'll pass in decline as
Orders for ramrod and nipple wrench amass and
    Redefine how responders take aim on the
Muzzleloading black-powder active shooter.
    We'll then party with fellow citizen gun lovers,
Glossing their shine in context line by line.

Hypno-cycloptic Box

The locus of American intolerance birthed anew
In th-age of television, a device that's separated
Us further than already from past perfect verbs

TOP DOWN
Keep 'em sated on sugar and lies and
Everything under the sun flies and
Dollar signs flash in their eyes while
They sing jingles of Colas & Moon Pies:

BOTTOM UP
Entranced as children they hooked us good
Like a prong in the gill we took the bait
Couldn't wait when home from school we'd
Turn on the set and begin to drool the
Resounding theme and the cast we adored
 Interlude then for ice cream
 And Wow our favorite cow Elsie
 Said kids it's not a dream

OMNICIENT EDITOR

Yeah, it was a nightmare, and it remains to train brains

    Mantras of mindlessness of media roil

    Enchanted a nation with gibberish, snake oil

    The piper's song drew them along and so arranged

    For whole communities to become estranged,

Neighborhoods where they'd goofed and played

The way kids do when they're easy with others

Across the tracks or over there around the back

Mixed colors & words traded laughed at or shaded, but

    All that began to slide with

           the advent of TV Guide -

they'd still hang awhile for a joke or a toke, but then

All would hit for home

To catch Gunsmoke

Interleaved with Pavlov's rhymey ranting

Soon to be all over mom and dad, panting

Like dogs for the latest, the greatest thrill,

Hooked in the gill

Exceptional Messages

American exceptionalism has long been a song
we've forced nations to sing along, never mind
its arhythmic thrum, God is a rule of thumb we
continually conduct yet no longer does it sound, as
fealty to Money has yielded the high moral ground,

Of course, anyone paying attention would've long
been aghast at engineered racial hatred's bête noire,
human beings brought here chained in ships to the
shores of a great nation as in-human cargo trade;
industrial whips made slave to economic retrograde,

But nations that knew were involved in slavery too!
The Atlantic and Pacific oceans saw us separate unto
ourselves to butcher natives that assisted or resisted
land grab's expansive spark ignited by Lewis and Clark,
sentencing the rest to reservations at Uncle Sam's behest,

Whether manifest destiny was real or bogus, ship after
ship brought emigres promised a chance romance of the
soil, start anew where land was cheap, and bromide sold
countless the idea that their toil would bring them gold by
working hard; a lucky few the public knew by that canard,

Faiths, ethnicities we welcomed All to agree that we were
a land of the tolerant and the free as advertised diplomacy
via commerce, and embassies established worldwide the

ideal that American democracy offered rare transparency,
a beacon of light that stood above the plight of civil strife,

Decade upon decade we'd sold by then a well-told story,
Pulled up by the bootstraps Oh say can you see success
through pride in emerging literary strides, lore began as
never before the slogan land of milk & honey tapping the
identities of Hiawatha, Paul Bunyan, and Johnny Appleseed!

Africans & Irish shipped west by droves to breed upon the
land and to fornicate. My great, great grandfather and his
brother numbered among the horde history may relate, and
they melded into a garden-variety wagon wheel reference as
though a rainbow appeared in a visionary kind of state....

Decade upon decade would the officious story flow....

By the 1960s the myth began to unravel when dissent
over Vietnam saw massed protest marchers gassed as
cops beat freedom to assemble in the street to repeat
raised voices against a war by warrior drumbeat cant,
"The whole world is watching!" heard Chicago chant!

Ritualistic peans to greatness's tarnished grace, like a
mirror cracking as you study that oft painted trace, there
were wake-up calls that all wasn't right, but the mighty
dollar you couldn't scream louder the way it saved face;
America braced for the fall by ignoring its own local call.

By then Green Go was in every Latin American land alert
to quell we like to tell but also to instigate upon demand
disruption over political assignment unless that State went
to the fold of the original idea sold that we master their
ways unto ours, think of a skin graft or eyeball alignment.

Having gained the world stage, it's damned hard to exit at
our age whether one is or is not bereft at the separation
perceived, having sung bogus soliloquies old and new,
whose lyrics bear scant relation to the state of the nation as
seen from abroad; an old benefactor viewed as malefactor?s

We're world-class experts at elusive public relations led by
the dollar Ka'ching! like a ring run thru the nose of an ox:
Sales of freedom is a theatre of actors, roles, masks. To
entice an audience isn't enough, you must lure to that bed
whole honey-hive sex-drive obscuring the glaring paradox!

Carbon Ogre Friday, or A Visit from Mom

~ pre ~

Slept poorly last night, morning
muscle cramp soreness pervades
while smoke from forest fires in
Oregon & California blown north
shroud the city as I drag my carapace
through a visual zombie apocalypse

"Well, isn't this a fine how do you do?"

1.

Looking out the windows
it's easy to imagine a planet's demise
when one cannot view, much less surmise,
expected daily sunrise, this day dawned subsumed
in blankets of smoke!

Old Mom Nature strides along, Her
grey cloak trailing, She's come once
again to chide the humans at their failing,
"Now children, look what you've done!"
While She knows Her lessons ring hollow: what
She *can* do after centuries of industrial spew
that one thing is clear,
by raising temps She dilates our level of fear!

2.

In the old days of the last century
night would bring lower temps &
higher humidity—working all out
day and night in the roaring fight
the jumping orange blaze and heat
who the hell noticed other than line
boss or food crew back at fire camp

~ ~ time travel ~ ~

Sitting in their churches appointed
formal in sparkling livery purchase
evangelicals declaim the End you see
is near we must suspend all Liberty
to acts of prayer: and self-flagellation
will bring an end to the conflagration

In the old days of the last century
night would bring lower temps and
higher humidity, on small fires you'd
feel the damp & hope would rise from
line boss to every fart sack in fire camp
then it's time to put that mother down
piss bags back up bang! Pulaski sound

~ ~ time travel ~ ~

Singing in their ironclad churches
formal in sparkling livery purchase
evangelicals declaim The End revealed
so must suspend all Liberty appealed
to acts of prayer: for self-flagellation
will bring some end to conflagration

~ in situ ~

In the new days of the new century
climate change has dried the fuels &
outdistanced fire knowledge rules,
burned pages from the old playbook,
all that jazz out the window; dreams of
night humidity now a specious perfidy

Our days and nights will be of smoke
the yellow of sun the green of trees a
bitter joke, and few will tell how well it
was before when every signal bore the
signs you could sense within the breeze
while science was ignored for the lord

~ in toto ~

Distraught in their burnable churches
informal in Salvation Army purchase
evangelicals decamp and wail the end
a stamp upon the soul of rigamarole
as others join supremacist cults no less

certain of thunder's almighty results

~ refrain ~

The new days of new century woes,
climate change has dried the fuels, far
outdistanced fire knowledge rules, and
the old playbook's pages have burned
all that puff jazz out the window goes,
night humidity will now be spurned

~ post ~

Now, as we see, it did not end well,
in 2020's heavy smoke cloak smell
visibility maybe a quarter mile &
COVID-19 all the fearful while as
magic thinkers dropped like flies
chanting Satan vaccination lies,

While Mom taught the Rules as one more
Warning made to us money-lust fools

Offend Me!

for LWP Ross

Honored are not the *words* themselves;
     it's the aural insult fielded toughens the HIDE, to
Sling One Back, like you know, *jerk wad*
     that one's been around since forever

Any guy calls me a *fag* I dig it! At the hmm
     least some guy is drawn to drawing
comparisons is all they are, and hey,
     complementary ears will tell you how
to banter along the way true tough stuff does!

          {Spoken Visayan and Tagalog in the room erupts,
               ears follow invective lilts & thick skin laughter}

Privilege breeds intolerance is the message
     we get before true colors bleed through and
those folks you thought you knew spew verbal
     dreck all over you from their upstaged defense!

          {Don't be slack Jack, sling it back!}

These days we take too much give too little back
inborn, inchoate, insipid attention lack, riveted to
money's vulgar dredges beneath hope of learning,
as opposed to true language users & lingo realists

hitting a nail on the head, calling a spade a spade
by using relative usable terms such as *blind*,
Change it, and the blind can't lead the blind up a blind
alley on a blind date on blind faith or blind luck -
Must duck hunters exclaim they bagged a brace of mallards
            behind a duck visually impaired?
        Visually impaired means you're useless without your
            Coke-bottle glasses, four-eyes!
        Visually impaired equals hangovers so fierce your
            vision sizzles with each exhalation!

Do I offend by using a verb you don't like? An adverb?
Prepositions done you wrong all along only now disturb?

    Please, I *beg* you to offend me!

    C'mon, *offend me*
        DO IT!

Being offended makes you tough, and far
tougher than the language you gargle daily
that owns your ability to say you are Free,
as I can't tell you how many halfwits hold
forth in offense-offered toxic venal-radio
hallways at all hours of the day and the night!

Please call me Asshole, or Bitch, or Cunt
so I can field them on the fly to better wield
the way of compliment or of complement if
words are meant as a role, an itch, or a stunt.

When I was a kid kids taunted each other (mercilessly),
    Sticks and stones can break my bones but
WORDS will never hurt me! Learned words listen:
        it's better to be stung, there's no
        other way to know the stinger!

I want you to call me Dago, or an E____, or Fatty,
(if you can think of an offensive word beginning
with the vowel /e/ .... Gee, would Elephant Ass do?)
I want you to say it to me loud & clear and
        lean in with derisive leer to inure to toughen
hides so lacking in today's lily- livered whining-American
    two-legged invertebrates

                HEY!

We strive to be Considerate of Others and Respectful;
    The Golden Rule is the Number One Tool we use to
Deal with systemic intolerance in the real!
    But forced language change to make that
Arrange only admits us to the zoo; you gotta know
    Reverse evolution will never be the solution:

The fate of PC language and woke, too, no doubt
Is that original meaning got turned inside out
To be rebranded for marketplace clout; and new

Hate-Woke assembly is cheap ad copy news as
It goosesteps down the avenues, and in schools
Marches us down the hallway to see the Principal,
Mr. Fascism.
'We will not tolerate such thinking young man/woman/bot
                Keep it up, be aberrant and by gosh
                before how long we'll no longer
                tolerate parents or parenting!'

Reworked woke may aim to neuter a suitor like a dog where
Juliet's balcony speech, Wherefor art thou Romeo, is heard as
            AI-generated stress & tone free monologue!

One sure way out of the semantic drone cult
            is to call a spade a spade.

            Language *does* change all on its own replete with
            New lexemes added as others go obsolete:

William Shakespeare's Middle English provides
                an eclectic example.
    Elizabethan curse words have been long out of use,
                but hey, you can
        Find them, they are not obtuse, thou peasant Swain,
                whoreson malthorse drudge!

Perhaps here's the solution to our Sensitivity Pandemic, we
   Rutted, crook-pated canker-blossoms;
  We frothy toad-spotted scuts! Admit the bunch of us are
    beslubbering beef-witted maggot pies!
Spleeny onion-eyed pigeon eggs!
Clot-poles! Hedge-pigs!
Rump-fed puttocks!

Of our corrected language fever,
our roots not in cahoots, and if
self-aware would choose to sever

 I Demand you call me any recently molded in-or-
out-of-lexicon-embrace like what was the last
one we thought we'd die laughing over how brazen
everyone gets in breathless cancel culture caress?

How did growing measures of depth & weighty aural
meaning not reveal universally unreported brain swelling
pursuant to grunts and keening elementals for evening
as we skirt around the berm of historical precedent?

Good question, yet it hangs as useless utility livery
in the absence of someone calling me a hunchback! or

any repartee where we shoot, you know, shit,
about forefathers dragging out grandfathered-in
grandmothers
to drum that wampum into honesty's faceless ego!

Poseidon Vinyl Chloride

Sailing west through the Strait of

      Juan de Fuca close hauled in our Fowlies,
Passing Victoria Island to starboard on
Our fiberglass vessel stuffed to the scuppers
      with months of food containers.
      Wherever will the empties go?
      Well, I think you know. Some
Forty years ago, Allen Ginsberg wrote in
'What the Sea Throws Up at Vlissingen,'
      a poem listing human dreck
      manufacture production output direct, a
Harbinger of throwaway culture's
Tidal toilet dynamo, a world of
      Consumerism
Unchecked material splendor elastic
    Perpetual spew of plastic
    from a colossal blender.
Passing Cape Flattery to port
    into the chop and thrill we
Enter the Western Liquid Plastic Dump
Where flotsam collection by wind driven current
      is churned by the plant's undercurrent, and here
        we offer offer Homage to

Poseidon Vinyl Chloride by

Jettisoning a mostly empty jug of Tide, then

On a beam reach we beam with glutton pride –

    Moving the fairlead forward to induce heel

We sail on the rail

    To empirically feel the thrill!

Sailing a sea of our human swill!

Proposal to Make the Great Pacific
Garbage Patch an American State
"Wedgies float back from reefs made of jeeps: more offshore debris."
Kenward Elmslie

Haphazard have been the efforts to clean up the Great Pacific
Garbage Patch refuse - news lag consigned to slag - What's App
remains obtuse, but then our daughter saw it,

       Look Mom!

A floating plastic dispatch bag with Target logo headed for the
shipping channel in the Strait of Juan de Fuca, Pacific bound:

An exuberant is out there Right Now on a trust fund trimaran 60
fielding a Hoover the size of a blue whale. A question that remains
is where does one dump when the bag is full, nozzle choked and
howling in squall while we ignore who's keeping score, and ask
what's in it for us if we could undo our consumerist glut?

Fishing gear lost at sea & trash dumped from ships,

navies and merchant fleets have no place

to come to grips, but our free market

human outflow is really the issue

more than attempts to vacuum, even if

it's worth the try; how to reign in industry

While countries along the Pacific Rim throw

wholesale into the sea, the United States,

largest production amount of plastic trash
per capita of any country wherever you go:
we're brash at 270 pounds per person per-
Anum on a scale that increasingly escalates

Halfway between California and Hawaii,
And Twice the size of Texas, consider a
high standard of living, lusty taxes
if we made the garbage Patch a U. S.
State, we as volume consumers can relate
to *soil* made from what we despoil

At 88,000 tons you'd think it could be
swirled in toward land close enough
in shore to add fill until it's tough;
See, we'd anchor from giant barges
pontoon scaffolds at varying depths;
cabled together the foundation enlarges

Ocean plastic trash breaks down
but never decomposes. Might seal
the better deal to glue it together,
spray it with grass seed from hoses
while amassing more trash until the
property meets our can-do measure

After all, we're an ingenious lot,

Suppose we who invented plastic

came up with an aggregate less drastic

from out of the melting pot engineer stew,

new space made from old waste, marine replace,

making swill by high tech gear to floating landfill

At first it might be spongy underfoot like some

yards in Belize where crabs dig as they please, but

models like this will show the way to make a State,

most likely to expand and prosper until easement

curtails sprawl and paves the way for ad campaigns

barking boating luxury mooring seaside real estate

Proposed:

   Make the Great Pacific Garbage Patch a U.S. State

                Sovereign – the United Nations weighs in

                   Binding upon swearing

               Decreed and signed & other dictates,

           Regulations same as all maritime states

Yes, the 51st State, and Puerto Rico can be 52 or fight:
               (banner slogan overnight!)

           One, a mushy state by trash contained, the
           Other repeatedly trashed by hurricane

Of course,

laggards will lag, pull ugly faces at

        Environmental regs in places

Where cash flow suffers from ill-gotten health

Amid the wars of internecine wealth, while the

United Nations discusses the state of oceans,

Bankers & investors gnash teeth and clash:

Win the bidding war and claim your isle of trash!

Reading poetry at Somethyme

for the Spirit of Aden Field

Pot walloping in steam blast sinks

with shouting cooks & the offhand

curse made fertile for writing verse

Once, discussing with Aden Field

and others the summons to poems

in that alcove just off the kitchen,

      forward of the toilets,

      wood slat wall in back,

I weighed in that I didn't call myself a

poet because I seemed to flutter in the

prop wash stream indistinctly between

avocation and vocation,

      at which point Aden

      lit into me, but no

dressing down,

more like squaring things to shape,

easy to deal with in plebian terms.

This standout memory survives due to a

parallel that year and Aden's reprise,

an open forum and a poet named Feather at

the COSMEP conference in Chapel Hill.

That wasn't a dressing down either, more like
a public stripping of that stippling faux Keats;

      constructive criticism

      to the open ears

      gains foresight foremost

      through hindsight gears.

Veteran of Peace

To my ex) military friends, this may help you
Grasp the swerve of those who chose not to serve
in the armed forces:
We're not veterans of war. We are veterans of <u>Peace</u>!
Some of us left home as teenagers because we got kicked out by
Our fathers who refused to acknowledge the times a-changing;
For some of us, that footloose freedom was an adventure.
For others, there was the fear we
Might get drafted and sent to
Some war by warriors crafted.
We loved our country, but we didn't believe
the hype over 'Nam' communism stereotype.
We hoped like hell we wouldn't be sent to
The four corners of the world
    to kill people
That Richard Nixon said a threat to the
Security of the greatest nation on earth [Stet] but for
Many, Dean Smith's Four Corners was good enough!
For others, it was Positively 4th Street.
We heard Dylan, Ochs, Baez, in-listening otherwise
Their anti-war songs became our anthems.
We made lasting friendships in the peace movement.
We made brothers and sisters.

We made love, not war.

We joined hands in a nation-wide movement.

We cheered on our heroes such as Allen Ginsberg, the Berrigans,

The Catonsville Nine.

We attended teach-ins against the war.

We attended anti-war protest planning sessions.

We marched (down Main Street) in Moratorium parades.

We attended anti-war protests that were peaceful.

We attended anti-war protests that were not peaceful.

No one I knew behaved violently, but

We got caught up in it.

We got chased by riot-squad cops.

We got walled in by phalanx of Billy clubs.

Some of us got tear-gassed, others got beaten.

Some of us got arrested.

Some of us got interviewed.

Some of us ducked into alleys for a breather, or a joint.

We participated in time-honored pacifist rituals

Strengthening our bonds and camaraderie.

We mourned as one over the Kent State murders.

We burned as one with immolated Buddhist monks.

We reeled in horror over the Mi Lai Massacre, then in stunned

silence when there was no accountability:

Killers ran free from their butchery!

We felt as one for civilians, as well for combatants

Caught in the haze of Agent Orange.

Most importantly,

We saw our collective action
Help to end that stupid war's intractable infraction.
We empathized with those among us
Who got drafted and went along with it,
Like a buddy of mine who lost his deferment.
He told them he intended to return to complete an
Engineering degree, so they made him a clerk in
An engineering battalion, and he spent his war
Typing and delivering the mail.
The coolest thing is that he doesn't brag grand
Service performed for his country; he put it all behind him
While he finished growing up (warzone-stunted hormones).

We met again at the Desert Storm anti-war rally
    (So many more since it is tough to tally),
The faces of our family, true patriots all, were all
Gathered again and freezing on the National Mall.
We didn't stop that war, but hey, at least we tried,
Burnishing to gloss America's Other Side bona fide.

My Search for the lost Ancient Asshole Mine

When echoes enter to fill the silence,

Pray, let 'em roam about the childless home,

then let be. We do not all arrive in

Measured grace and granted gold,

Some suffer and others suffer worse;

    That's the way it is, the way it's been.

        I'd hoped to visit my great cubed Grandfather's

Homeplace by carrying tradition in

My arms, but I miscalculated the

Calcium deficiency in war time,

As well as the malignant record-

keeping of maintaining abuse

Ledgers gone to the illustrated

Manuscripts of dust obtuse,

        Things go awry they always do

For some of us; my father didn't

Know his father and that father

While fathering didn't preserve

So much as a winking notion,

Bones gone to powder

Blowing in the wind, or

On a shelf somewhere nowhere and

That says it all right there. In a

Field teeming with ancestry freaks

that charge for the glory of their expertise,

Bona Fide is chiseled away to bogus fide

in a gambling of epic proportions, if

only some numb nuts would anthologize:

Grand Avalanche of Family Dung

fed by rivers engorged by springs by pools

from attic storage & stowage, the photogravure

sepia stare of a future they were unaware.

You'd mean nothing to them

in your postmodern utilities, it's that disconnect

explains why you're such an ugly fucker.

Affluence grows Effluence floes

1.   Chemicals of 'emerging concern' quote unquote
Are flowing into Puget Sound, according to a
Southern Resident Orca toxicologist who
Prefers the pod to remain anonymous.

Wastewater graywater, call it what you like,
Flowing creeping seeping population sprawl
Chemicals in the hundreds lacing fish tissue,
Antibiotics, lipstick, mascara; no fright wigs yet

But just you wait. The poorly evolved humanimal,
That obstreperous two-legged dung beetle, too often
Flushes old medicine down toilets, or they own lotions
When talking to God on the big white telephone

When chinook salmon were sought for quips
Few could be found without Estee Lauder lips!

2.   I've spilled leaded boat gas
             From the spill-proof safety can
       The most complicated device
             Ever designed by unkind man

I've spilled boat soaps

      Runaway suds astride the tide,

Lubricant too, drops plop then spread

      The curse, the guilt, *that* abide

I've watched ships jettison shits,

      Offshore is often too soon inshore,

Gaia's toilet the mindset fits

      Capital commerce from store to store

I'd like to honor Any Boater,

      Without mishap or chemical floater,

We go where our ablative bottoms

      Will take us; is it truly any wonder

Orcas would forsake us?

Every time it rains, fish who are living

      Downstream of storm drains are

Exposed to all the pollutants given by we

      Driven two-legged mutants

Massive die-offs of Coho salmon and

      Now some trout have joined the ranks:

Urban mortality runoff syndrome, to

Modernization we must give thanks?
Why not establish permanent care
For our increasingly fragile habitat
And Walk the Walk that lays it bare
That Living Love is where it's at!

Precis: Capitalism Jism, or
Uncle Sam's Greed Seed

"The democracy of today holds the liberty of one man to be absolutely
nothing when in conflict with another man's right of property."
– Abraham Lincoln, 1859

Bear in mind while reading here

Anything gilded is just veneer;

Beneath the glitter & the gold

A tale of inequality unfolds:

Ruining lives to save a dime

Sums the mammon paradigm

Disclaimer

A nation is made Great by a Great people.

Great people are defined by Great deeds,

Selfless and Noble, Humanitarian in Scope,

Teaching Integrity while Offering Hope,

Extending Ethics of the Golden Rule and

Sharing Among Others that Generous Tool

Such countries exist, but
this one's not on the list

The United States talks the talk

43

Spreading the message, 'we are free,'

Yet we fail utterly to Walk the Walk of a

Democracy; instead, we grow a money

Tree that's watered by Created Poverty

In 2018, just two percent (2%) of the U.S. Congress came from the

Working Class!

Is anyone surprised that our national government is so comprised?

Folks from the working class can't spare the time off the

Assembly Lines,

Although now and again a grass-roots run is spun just to

Show to anyone that Yes, it can be done, but generally,

It's only the wealthy who may so avail of the

Time to spend on the gladhanding campaign trail.

18th Century

"A democratic society puts a premium on equality; a capitalist economy
does not." - Lewis Lapham

Gentlemen farmers and the well-to-do made up

the Continental Congress, with few, if any,

Cotton picker servant class amid all that inherited wealth

{Patrick Henry & Samuel Adams were the standout threadbare

exceptions to that inaugural unrepresentative rule: we mark them

for their words, their deeds, but shun their bona-fide poverties}.

Let's take a look back, see what we can see in the

Grisly mirror of American class division glass:

{This review won't attempt to eschew God Greed's

Greatest sin, American slavery at its origin, rather to

Attest the font from whence the greed seed flows}

Thomas Paine and his common man were distrusted by

Thomas Jefferson's fellow landed-gentry clan, to them,

Liberty meant the freedom to hold estates, not the

Rights of people or the equality that might create.

Aghast at Pennsylvania's state constitution draft as too

Democratic, the framers knew the document they'd craft:

A blend of Aristotle and English philosopher John Locke;

Oligarchy first, then a Bill of Rights to pacify the flock

19th Century

"If the United States ... are also to grow vast crops of poor, desperate,
dissatisfied, nomadic, miserably-waged populations, such as we see
looming upon us of late years-steadily, even if slowly, eating into them
like a cancer of lungs or stomach-then our republican experiment,
notwithstanding all its surface-successes, is at heart an unhealthy failure."
— Walt Whitman, 1879

In mining history, when workers were repeatedly brutalized

By penny wages, hovels worse than cages, hours without end,

Miserable miners who'd had enough organized to amend any

Hope for decency. But petitions for leniency got them beaten!

The loudest were stilled after wives and shacks attacked; kids

Fared no better, many were killed by vigilantes hired by mine

Owners; the *audacity* that Profit Margins be mired, and more,

That peons from shackles be freed offended the God Greed!

Working for a living and doing your best is a challenge

Unchanged since the Pilgrims brought the east to the west;

Hardscrabble yarns and homespun tales abound of that test

To make a homestead prosper. Where clamor for empire?

1873:

Corporate railroad companies reduced worker pay

By ten percent to protect their profits one day as the

Long Depression held sway (1873-79). Four years on,

Ten percent again while they cut the labor force low

Brought work to a roundhouse standstill at the B&O: No

Train would run 'til the cut's annulled, the harm undone.

The contempt wealth breeds for anything less refused to

Negotiate to clear up the mess, instead brought in federal

Guns to oppose the strikers and make the trains again run,

But the strike had spread, and to the north and east it led to

Include the Pennsylvania Railroad, to factories and to mills

    And to cities spread far and wide across the hills;

    It's said some hundred thousand workers tried to

Shift for better conditions as the jails filled, and

Some hundred or more of 'em had been killed.

While politicians hawed on about labor reform,

Little was done and they soon restored the norm

That has persisted through the ages, busting up

Unions, the heartless cutting of workers' wages

1890:

Draft animals, describes steel workers in any of

Dale Carnegie's mills; twelve-hour shifts seven days a

Week every week and one day off (July 4th) per year,

Seen as the highest praise of steel refining efficiency

No breaks for meals reveal steel's efficiency peak, as

The average worker made maybe ten dollars a week;

Five hundred dollars earned per year for life, is it any

Wonder that the *Gilded Age* premiered labor strife?

Refrain

Money culture money will never fill a till

Conveyor-belt feeds of human toil attest,

Greed feeds from every blood bank landfill

Vested fund waves hedged never to crest

1892:

Well known was Carnegie's projected public pro-labor stance

But it devolved to a fictional embrace of an ugly romance

When he went after one mill's union when steel prices fell;

He created for Homestead an epic battle and a raging hell.

    The company dug in and with paid political aid

    Brought in scab labor to wield the spade, and

    Were donated federal troops by lackeys on a pad;

    Before long, the strikers knew they'd been had

    Refrain (Top-down Disdain)

    How dare my employees beg me for a dime

    Ingrates don't know when they got it good;

    My private police will treat it as a crime, and

    My newspapers will hail me Robin Hood

An elderly philanthropist is how Carnegie's known, who

Gave away fortunes from his own pennies grown, but

He'd starve all his workers to spite a rival; look it up,

His Machiavellian brutality to suffering is archival!

    Why is it we honor and treasure rags-to-riches

with so many textbook *heroes* as sons-of-bitches?

1898:

The Western Federation of Miners ranks quickly grew

When non-union miners demanded union scale too.

A meagre .50 per hour would give them better pay,

But the market for silver had gone astray and was

Just then in a rut, some claimed due to a supply glut.

Bunker Hill & Sullivan Mining Company cried foul &

Avowed not to raise the wage so much as a sliver;

{picture gelatinous jowls aquiver}

Profit margins under threat reveal their callow

Refusal to deal with diggers in their holes as they

Hired Pinkerton detectives undercover as moles.

While local business urged them to pay union scale;

Bunker Hill's response: get back to work or go to jail, but

Undaunted, union men hijacked a train and with it blew up

The housing where (seen as rats) Pinkerton sleuths remained

As well as machinery for milling or refining the ore, but the

Company's political connections by then evened the score,

Bringing in federal troops and martial law so as to tame any

Chances of meaningful change, and wages remained the same.

Degraded miners brought violence, to be sure, but it

Was met ten times over that Dominance Endure.

Note that in each labor dispute

industrialists and their likes were

gifted private cops of ill repute,

infamous for busting strikes[1]

Pooling companies made the corporate tycoon

Who gambled it all and shot for the moon on

The backs of impecunious sweat, blood, and toil;

God Greed thus arose to pillage and despoil as

Carnegie and Morgan (et. al) held forth the trowel

Building the foundation walls of corporate power,

Buying their way upward to the governing tower

    {a nascent hobby that begat the Lobby}

And paving the way for men like Lewis Powell

Their refusal to discuss labor issues and negotiate,

Escalating worker despair while invigorating ire,

Established the benchmark God Greed's prelate

Set to torch trade unions and stoke the fire

Refrain (Omnipotent)

    Looking askance at the 'Gilded Age'

    Amassing great fortunes was all the rage

    Got by paying labor an inhuman wage;

    Along with the rise of corporate patricians

    Enter corrupted bought & paid-for politicians

These so-called titans, or with the pilot designation,

'Captains of Industry,' are idolized in blind elation.

    Why aren't we aghast over their crass negations

Of human decency in working class relations?

Drumbeats of adulation that cadenced the norm

Denied (degraded) labor a savior and so crushed reform

Encore

Almost a given was the nation's Credit Mobilier scandal in

Which Union Pacific Railroad brass got a choke-hold handle —

Not a labor dispute, although labor was there to be milked —

With inflated costs, shadow expenses and fraudulent contracts

Bilked the Federal treasury $44 million with invented facts —

In due course endemic racism would a rabid press ensure

That a gullible public took and would for long obdure;

Anything native to this land would be driven to expire that

Great God Greed may run rampant and in dollar lust desire:

And all this while out West a travesty unfolded at our behest:

> Because they were not 'improving their land,'
> Native Americans lost theirs to white demand
> That proceeded to topple above, mine below but
> Attention drawn to Buffalo Bill's Wild West show

> Original Americans were ousted to reservations,
> As a cold war engaged in human degradations
> Until discovery of minerals beneath their lands
> When those too were stolen by White demands.

Rutherford B. Hayes, 1886:

"This is a government of the people, by the people and
or the people no longer. It is a government by the corporations, of
the corporations and for the corporations."

20<u>th</u> Century

"We may have democracy, or we may have wealth concentrated in the hands of a few, but we can't have both." – Louis Brandeis

1.

The capitalist century got off with a Bang and

Among those that fell when the shots rang,

Eleven children whose bodies then burned in the

Tent colony at Ludlow that God Greed spurned.

Eleven thousand miners went on strike against the

Rockefeller family's feudal system of low pay and

Dangerous working conditions in every way; the

Miners were repaid with eviction from their shacks

But that was only the opening act of a cataract as

Tent colonies arose upon the hills, helped by the

United Mine Workers Union, continued to picket

Over which Rockefeller sent in his hired thugs

On an armored train with Gatling guns, they fired

At will as though they were out to hunt and kill

Their fellow man, and they bagged 26 yet weren't

Able to rid the nuisance, and the strike went on

Unwilling to take it anymore, Rockefeller aimed to

Settle the score and as a reward his pal the Governor

Gave him the National Guard that in trade set up

Machine guns to enfilade prior to setting ablaze

The tents and shelters where women and children

Cowered and where many of them were murdered.

Violence then spread in every direction and killing

Was general and on each side many more died

Heroic was the stand of 82 Guardsman who refused

To board a troop train headed for the melee on the

Grounds that they would not freely participate in

The wanton killing of women and children

Demonstrations deluged the capitol; editorials called

The Governor the accessory that he was, and 400

United Garment Workers women volunteered as

Nurses to offer aid and assistance to the strikers, and

After that protests spread across the nation 'til Federal

Troop immersion sent by President Wilson, interrupting his

Mexico Diversion, shut it down; 66 had died in that time, but

Not a single Guardsmen was ever indicted for their crime[2]

2.

J. Edgar Hoover's Feds destroyed the labor unions to

Thwart the leftists of their ambitious political footings

But so doing let in the dogs of organized crime, then

Looked the other way; that legacy's still with us today,

In the concept that laborers have no worth beyond

What they produce; their time has no value but the

Bottom Line; they're expendable; send 'em packing;

Send their jobs overseas: Anything to feed God Greed

The American Extreme pursuit of profit at the

Expense of all else human and divine defines a

Callow Heartless Hard-bitten Raw sampled apple

From the poisoned vine of the American Dream

Refrain

To pay the bills Jacks & Jills climb hills

Laboring up Sisyphus Street they go, its

Clockwork task devoid of frills but with

Dreams delayed & hungry kids in tow.

>Those who bought the headphone packet? After Select click *Support Your Family Racket* as we view the exhibit:

"At no moment in its history has America declared lasting peace between the haves and the have nots. Temporary cessations of hostility, but no permanent closing of the social and moral divide between debtor and creditor, and no giving up on the thought that some lives matter more than others."[3]

Through the 1920s & 30s capitalism had labor in its sights: 80

Million per-anum[4] for anti-union skulkduggery by hundreds of

Detective firms – one wonders, were the gumshoe & shamus too

Treated like shit, but given the high pay they could not forfeit?

From the era of the Works Progress Administration and the

Second New Deal, the fight against greed would rise and fall

But never fully succeed, while corporate antipathy begat anti-

Union law firms pitting the suits against the dungaree lunchpail

Crowd to enforce the credo: pay the lowest wage then hold 'em

In contempt if they attempt to engage mastery of their station via

Litigation, and that situation remains static to this reading but for

Shipping of jobs overseas, the global sweatshop disease, and that

Invasive species, Lobbying, treading softly the halls of Congress

While carrying the big stick of perverse commerce[*] and the pledge

Allegiance to gluttonous need to feed God Greed the breadth of

The North American heartland from Amazon to Zappos

-Commercial Break-

Now, there's nothing awry over making a buck;

Companies that respect people over profit tend to

Maintain a happy-to-be-there workforce, such a

Simple equation's bottom line is bedrock ethics!

Stellar among them is the worker-owned enterprise
And the not-for-profit business model, one that's
Thumbing its nose everywhere God Greed goes to
Piss on labor and dock the pay of time-clock cattle.

*Egregious examples of perverse commerce:

>In 1989 the oil tanker Exxon Valdez hit a reef in Alaska's
Prince William Sound, covering 1200 miles of shoreline with oil.
"The man left at the helm, the third mate, would never have hit the
Bligh Reef had he simply looked at his Raycas radar. But he could
not, because the radar *was not turned on*. The complex Raycas system
costs a lot to operate, so frugal Exxon management left it broken
and useless."[5]

>Between 1970 and 1979 the Ford Motor Company
produced cars with a defective automatic transmission design that
could not be firmly placed in the park position; it was easily
bumped or jarred into reverse gear, resulting in some ninety injuries
and deaths. Litigation established that Ford engineers had known
of the problem since 1971 but had done nothing to correct it. –

Ford also produced the notorious Pinto. They knew from crash
tests it would explode when rear-ended at speeds as low as 20 mph.
To fix the problem the company would lose $11.00 per car, but
they chose instead to ignore such costs. The eventual death toll
reached 180 with an equal number of drivers and passengers
suffering serious burns. Ford would wait another five years before
recalling more than a million of the deadly cars.[6]

21st Century

"Money has reckoned the soul of America." - Allen Ginsberg, 1959

"It's okay to be angry about Capitalism." – Senator Bernie Sanders, 2023

Now, since corporations are people too (Citizens United)

They'll pay taxes like the rest of us do on revenue? HAH!

    Fat Chance that romance will ever do more than

Screw the likes of me and you (as intended)

        Corporations use their tax-cut windfalls

        To buy back their own stock rather than

        Raising wages; that callow glib-slick worm

        On the baited hook a gullible public took

Amazon in 2022 spent more than $16 Million to

Fight against higher wages & better conditions.

Others seeking similar renditions that bleed labor for

Capital Greed number among such clusterfucks as

Apple, Google, Tesla, and Starbucks, and onward the

March of Woe in opposition to Labor upgrade goes at

Chipotle, McDonalds, REI (Really Expensive Inventory),

Trader Joe's (et. al)

Their hired union-busting firms strive to make inroads

Within the system lurking like worms or nematodes,

Invasion aimed at collective guts, no ifs, ands, or buts

Lobbyists & CEOs run the federal mills &

Elected officials sit as Representative shills

Feathering their nests and raking it in while

Selling us down the river on legislative spin.

    Let's hope we wake up before it's too late

    Like it oft seems to be for American labor.

Reject that God Greed will decide your fate!

Start up a business to support your neighbor!

Text notes

1 "Between 1866 and 1892, Pinkertons participated in 70 labor disputes and opposed over 125,000 strikes." pbs.org/wgbh/americanexperience/features/carnegie-strike-homestead-mill

2 Woody Guthrie: https://www.youtube.com/watch?v=XDd64suDz1A

3 Lapham's Quarterly, Democracy 2020

4 *From the Folks Who Brought You the Weekend: A Short, Illustrated History of Labor in the United States.* Priscilla Murolo & A.B. Chitty, New York: The New Press, 2001

5 *The Best Democracy Money can Buy: An Investigative Reporter Exposes the Truth About Globalization, Corporate Cons, and High-finance Fraudsters.* Greg Palast. New York: Penguin 2003

6 https://www.decof.com/documents/dangerous-products.pdf

Back in Chapel Hill

Holy shit!

    {He recalls when Dean Smith passed the crown, but

    here the milestone is the very face of the town!

Quaint got replaced by

                       nondescript as

Charm too got erased in that shift.

What paeon to Progress is this

                       soulless, forbidding

Iron-curtain architecture?

        This is no wistful look back,
        rather a screed given instant-
        ugly everywhere greed, bereft
        at a once personable town's
        character-killing identity theft

Looks like anywhere else now, save for

East Franklin Street's

One hundred block,

        still home to

Four Corners & the Carolina Coffee Shop, a must stop,

and Suttons Hamburger as Drug (Store), and also the

Varsity Theatre remains.

Perhaps such stalwarts

will never circle drains

thought the Davie Poplar,

as it watched me pass,

numberless alumnus yet

another season settle,

another leaf of grass

Last Words

I bit the hand that fed me,

and it slapped me upside

the head, and too soon

was seen

to kick vented spleen!

Drunken ranting bends the rules,

using friends as insult tools, but

retribution terrible & swift either

heals the wound or widens the rift

Taking of vows to never again

dump on scared cows

is often too little too late appealed;

friendships end, and fate is sealed

It takes a singular fool to
Screw the Golden Rule!

Steven Mooney as a writer:

Poetry, *In Cellophane of Time, Poems 1973-1987*, Regulator Press;

Gunited States, Last Word Press 2023; Draft2Digital 2025,

Mapping the Tongue, self-published.

Memoir, *Kottke Oeuvre Skookum, 6 & 12-string Ears, Vignettes,*

1970-2019 Draft2Digital.com.

Short Fiction, *Legend of Hyper Bole and Other Stories.*

Draft2Digital.com

Miscellany: Biographical Sketches, Essays, Stories: *A Bref History*

of Absolute Meat, Draft2Digital.com

Novels, *Dalton Bourbonette*. Also, the comic-absurd literary trilogy,

Cutlass Wonders; *The Ageless of Aquarius*; and *Chronicle of an English*

Morpheme Addict under the series title, *A Measure of Poe & Three*

Quarters, a free download at Draft2Digital.com